SYMBOLICAL CONSCIOUSNESS

AMERICAN ACADEMY OF RELIGION
AIDS FOR THE STUDY OF RELIGION SERIES

Edited by
Gerald J. Larson

Number 4

SYMBOLICAL CONSCIOUSNESS:
A COMMENTARY ON *LOVE'S BODY*

by
William C. Shepherd

SCHOLARS PRESS
Missoula, Montana

SYMBOLICAL CONSCIOUSNESS:
A COMMENTARY ON *LOVE'S BODY*

by

William C. Shepherd

Published by

SCHOLARS PRESS

for

AMERICAN ACADEMY OF RELIGION

Distributed by

SCHOLARS PRESS
University of Montana
Missoula, Montana 59801

SYMBOLICAL CONSCIOUSNESS: A COMMENTARY ON *LOVE'S BODY*

by

William C. Shepherd

Copyright © 1976

by

AMERICAN ACADEMY OF RELIGION

Quotations from *Love's Body*, by Norman O. Brown. Copyright © 1966 by Norman O. Brown. Reprinted by permission of Random House, Inc. Vintage Books edition.

Library of Congress Cataloging in Publication Data
Shepherd, William C
 Symbolical consciousness.

(Aids for the study of religion series ; no. 4)
1. Psychoanalysis. 2. Brown, Norman Oliver, 1913- Love's body. I. Title. II. Series.
BF175.S495   150'.19'5   76-26582
ISBN 0-89130-083-X

Printed in the United States of America

Printing Department
University of Montana
Missoula, Montana 59801

For

MRS

TABLE OF CONTENTS

INTRODUCTION 1

CHAPTER I: THE EARLY BROWN. 7

CHAPTER II: BROWN: *LIFE AGAINST DEATH* 11

CHAPTER III: APOCALYPSE: THE PLACE OF MYSTERY IN
             THE LIFE OF THE MIND 29

CHAPTER IV: *LOVE'S BODY* 33

CHAPTER V: SYMBOLICAL CONSCIOUSNESS AND A CHOICE. . . .77

Introduction

"To explore is to penetrate: the world is the insides of the mother.... Already in childhood the symbolic equivalents for the inside of the mother's body are discovered in external objects, the toys. Growing up consists in finding new toys, new symbolic equivalents; so that in all our explorations we are still exploring the inside of our mother's body." (pp. 36-7)

"Having a soul, the hero with a thousand faces, is the same as having genital organization--to take the penis as the 'narcissistic representative of the total personality.'" (p. 51)

"The endless task: to achieve the impossible, to find a male female (vaginal father) or female male (phallic mother). It is to square the circle; to desire the pursuit of the whole in the form of dual unity or the combined object...." (p. 71)

"All work is women's work. Every commodity is, as Marx says, a fetish, that is to say a non-existent penis. An investment. From feudal investiture to capitalistic investment, the manufacture of clothes for their own sake, not to be worn but to be saved in the hope chest. Instead of fixed robes and roles, fashion design and the endless search for identity: new personalities from old, turn in last year's model." (p. 78)

"To make in ourselves a new consciousness, an erotic sense of reality, is to become conscious of symbolism. Symbolism is mind making connections (correspondences) rather than distinctions (separations). Symbolism makes conscious interconnections and unions that were unconscious and repressed." (pp. 81-2)

"Personality is persona, a mask. The world is a stage, the self a theatrical creation." (p. 90)

"It is not that children, neurotics, and primitives are so stupid as to be unable to discriminate between words and things; it is that they are not so repressed as to be unaware that personality is a social fiction, and a name a magical invocation of a particular role in the social drama." (p. 92)

"The body, like the body politic, is a theater; everything is symbolic, everything including the sexual act.... The function of the representative organ is to impersonate, incarnate, incorporate in his own body the body politic." (p. 131)

"The divorce between soul and body takes the life out of the body, reducing the organism to a mechanism, dead in itself but given an artificial life, an imitation of life, by will or power." (p. 138)

"To give up boundaries is to give up the reality-principle. The reality-principle, the light by which psychoanalysis has set its course, is a false boundary between inside and outside; subject and object; real and imaginary; physical and mental." (pp. 150-1)

"Literal meanings are icons become stone idols." (p. 185)

"Literal meanings as against spiritual or symbolic interpretation, a matter of Life against Death. The return to symbolism, the rediscovery that everything is symbolic--a penis in every convex object and a vagina in every concave one--is psychoanalysis. A return or turning point, the beginning of a new age (Aquarius?); the Third Kingdom, the age of the spirit prophesied by Joachim of Fiore; or the second coming, the resurrection of the body. It is raised as spiritual or symbolical body; the awakening to the symbolical life of the body." (p. 191)

"Literalism is to take pars pro toto; symbolism reconstitutes the lost (hidden) unity." (p. 210)

"In Ferenczi's apocalyptic theory of genitality the sexual act is a historical drama, a symbolic reenactment or recapitulation of all the great traumas in the history of the individual, of the species, of life itself. Psychoanalytic time is not gradual, evolutionary, but is discontinuous, catastrophic, revolutionary. The sexual act is a return to the womb." (p. 211)

"Literalism is idolatry, taking shadows for reality; taking abstractions, human inventions, unconscious projections of the human spirit, as autonomous power; letting the metaphors go dead, and then, when dead, bowing down before them, taking them literally." (p. 222)

"Overthrow the importance principle; turn it upside down. Put down the mighty from their seats, and exalt them of low degree. Every throne a toilet seat, and every toilet a throne.... The distinction between the sublime and the vulgar is abolished; sublimation is swallowed up in symbolism. As above, so below; go high-low every time. The way up is the way down; the penis a symbolic head, and vice versa." (pp. 236-7)

"A symbol is never a symbol but always polysymbolic, overdetermined, polymorphous." (p. 248)

"Symbolism is polymorphous perversity, the translation of all of our senses into one another, the interplay between the senses, the metaphor, the free translation. The separation of the senses, their mutual isolation, is sensuality, is sexual organization, is bondage to the tyranny of one partial impulse, leading to the absolute and exclusive concentration of the life of the body in the representative person." (p. 249)

"Symbolical consciousness, the erotic sense of reality, is a return to the principle of ancient animistic science, mystical participation, but *now for the first time freely*; instead of religion, poetry." (p. 254)

"The unspoken meaning is always sexual. Of sexuality we can have only symbolical knowledge, because sexual is carnal. Death and love are altogether carnal; hence their great magic and their great terror. Love that never told can be. It is the fool king Lear who asks his daughters to tell how much they love him. And it is the one who loves him who is silent." (p. 265)

"The antimony between mind and body, word and deed, speech and silence, overcome. Everything is only a metaphor; there is only poetry." (p. 266)

What are we to make of all that? To make something of it, I believe, will not be easy for any of us, but I also believe that making something of it is worth the trip. Everything dear is expensive. Religious texts frequently require and even demand non-literal interpretation. I warn you now that you will have to learn non-literal interpretation if you hope to benefit from Brown; for *Love's Body* does not allow *at all* for literalistic reading. There is no way to be literal about this book, and so we shall learn to be metaphorical, symbolical, figurative. And if we learn to do that we shall have learned Brown's major lesson.

I view my purpose in these pages, in metaphorical terms, as that of a traffic engineer: I offer some guideposts for the trip and I want to indicate where we have been coming from; I can also indicate what parallel roads run alongside ours.

A new perspective is imposed upon you by Norman O. Brown in *Love's Body*: he knows that the real is not the bare literal, not the simple descriptive, not, in Brown's phrase, the truth that any fool can see. Yet Brown's tradition is our own Western European one for the most part, the tradition that spawned Christianity, the tradition in which Christianity spawned science and thus became its own gravedigger, the tradition that spawned psychoanalysis and Marxism, and the tradition that has now laid itself open to a vast array of other traditions in a feverish quest to find itself. Perhaps we can better say: a feverish quest to lose itself in order to find itself. For Brown the most important of these other traditions is Buddhism. Finally we will be dealing with and in fact extending a quite individualistic tradition in pursuit of another, a different, a richer and deeper and more unified state of personal consciousness. Only thus, Brown argues, can we ever hope to save ourselves: even hope for the very survival of humanity today, he thinks, is a utopian one. And so we shall also be talking utopias.

Before I specify more exactly what I will be doing in these remarks, I want to mention another book and then some secondary literature on Brown for consultation should the need arise. First of all the book of Herbert Marcuse, *Eros and Civilization* (Random Vintage). I mention this because I will be spending some time here outlining the relationship between Marcuse and Brown, and their mutual relationships to the Marxist and Freudian traditions. So far as secondary literature is concerned, I urge caution: much of the writing about Brown and also Marcuse is ideological, some is simply wrong, much is harshly critical, some is naively and uncritically friendly, and some again is thoughtful and sincere, critical but cognizant of the enormous impact that the insights of especially Brown can have. But for a beginning I suggest Chapter III of Theodore Roszak's *The Making of a Counter Culture* (Doubleday Anchor): the chapter is titled "The Dialectics of Liberation: Herbert Marcuse and Norman O. Brown"--Roszak thinks of Brown and not Marcuse as the genuine revolutionary. Second I suggest Paul Robinson's comparison of Marcuse and

Brown in the Marcuse chapter of his book called *The Freudian Left* (Harper Torchbook); Robinson thinks of Marcuse and not Brown as the genuine revolutionary. And finally for a balanced and favorable discussion of *Love's Body* I suggest the review of Robert Bellah, found in his book *Beyond Belief: Essays on Religion in a Post Traditional World* (Harper).

    My immediate strategy is to sketch Brown's intellectual odyssey for you. I am taking this route because I don't think it is possible to understand *Love's Body* without some insight into the evolution of Brown's thought, particularly as it takes shape in an earlier book, published in 1959, called *Life Against Death: The Psychoanalytic Meaning of History* (Wesleyan). So I'll begin by saying something about the early Brown and his eventual move to Freudianism. Then I'll compare the Brown of *Life Against Death* with the Marcuse of *Eros and Civilization*, which will require an examination of the rudiments of both Marxian and Freudian theories of human nature and civilization. Then I shall briefly discuss a crucial transition piece in Brown's evolution, a Phi Beta Kappa oration given at Columbia in 1961: it's called "Apocalypse: The Place of Mystery in the Life of the Mind" (*Harper's Magazine*, May, 1961). Next, using this framework, we'll be able to understand and interpret some passages from *Love's Body*, perhaps some of those that formed the introduction to this book; and I'll end by offering an evaluation of *Love's Body* and say why I think it is important, not as academic trivia, but rather for the quality of all our lives.

I   The Early Brown

Everything about Brown's early career bespeaks the conventional, and I think that this fact is not unimportant, for Brown will eventually find himself arguing, as many others such as R. D. Laing do also, that it is precisely the conventional in Western society that is mad. (Are lies really just inoperative statements?) In any event, Brown did undergo a conventional academic regimen at Oxford and the University of Chicago, eventually gaining his Ph.D. at the University of Wisconsin. He has taught at Nebraska Wesleyan University, Wesleyan University, the University of Rochester, and most recently, since the breakthroughs represented by *Life Against Death* and *Love's Body*, at the University of California, Santa Cruz. Brown's field was Classics, and he brought to his study a Protestant dedication to hard work; he was accordingly, as these things go, a competent Classics scholar, writing articles and books such as *Hermes the Thief* (University of Wisconsin) in obeisance to standard academic tradition. (Publish or Perish. Or is it Publish and perish?) But the important thing for our purposes is that Brown was steeping himself all these years in the classical and eventually post-classical literature of the Western tradition, and to do the job he had Greek, Latin, German, French, Italian and Spanish for tools at his easy disposal. And all these years as well, a fuse was burning in Brown, which finally was ignited by his study of Freud during the fifties and which illumined the intellectual landscape in 1959 with the publication of *Life Against Death*, hardly the standard offering from your basic staid professor of Classics.

Let me quote from the Introduction to that book before I turn to an examination of Brown's version of Freudian analysis applied to our common civilizational ills.

> In 1953 I turned to a deep study of Freud, feeling the need to reappraise the nature and destiny of man. Inheriting from the Protestant tradition a conscience which insisted that intellectual work should be directed toward the relief of man's estate, I, like so many of my generation, lived through the superannuation of the political categories which informed liberal thought and action in the 1930's... Those of us who are temperamentally incapable of embracing the politics of sin, cynicism, and despair have been compelled to re-examine the classic assumptions about the nature of politics and about the political character of human nature. But, unless I am mistaken, the feeling that traditional schools of thought have become stereotyped and sterile is not limited to those with my kind of background. This book is addressed to all who are ready to call into question old assumptions and to entertain new possibilities. And since new ideas will not come if their entry into the mind is subject to conformity with our old ones and with what we call common sense, this book demands of the reader--as it demanded of the author--a willing suspension of common sense. The aim is to open up a new point of view. The task of judicious appraisal, confronting theoretical possibility with the stubborn facts of present events and past history, comes later.
>
> But why Freud? It is a shattering experience for anyone seriously committed to the Western traditions of morality and rationality to take a steadfast, unflinching look at what Freud has to say. It is humiliating to be compelled to admit the grossly seamy side of so many grand ideals. It is criminal to violate the civilized taboos which have kept the seamy side concealed. To experience Freud is to partake a second time of the forbidden fruit; and this book cannot without sinning communicate that experience to the reader.
>
> But to what end? When our eyes are opened, and the fig leaf no longer conceals our nakedness, our present situation is experienced in its full concrete actuality as a tragic crisis. To anticipate the direction of this book, it begins to be

> apparent that mankind, in all its restless striving and progress, has no idea of what it really wants. Freud was right: our real desires are unconscious. It also begins to be apparent that mankind, unconscious of its real desires and therefore unable to obtain satisfaction, is hostile to life and ready to destroy itself. Freud was right in positing a death instinct, and the development of weapons of destruction makes our present dilemma plain: we either come to terms with our unconscious instincts and drives--with life and with death--or else we surely die.
> (*Life Against Death*, pp. xi-xii)
>
> . . . .
>
> We are concerned with reshaping psychoanalysis into a wider general theory of human nature, culture, and history, to be appropriated by the consciousness of mankind as a whole as a new stage in the historical process of man's coming to know himself. (p. xiii)

Already Brown is beginning to sound pretty apocalyptic here; his tone is intense and, indeed, he is already beginning to play the role of a kind of revealer, which of course is the root meaning of the word apocalyptic. He tries to set out in *Life Against Death* not only a Freudian psychoanalytic theory to open a new perspective on the conflict-ridden relationship between individual selves and civilization; but, going far beyond that, he, unlike Freud himself, wants to offer a way out of the intensity of the conflict, to cure, in other words, our dis-ease. Where Freud saw only the possibility of tenuous and stoical resignation to the conflict between man's inner drives and the toll of civilization, Brown seeks to get at the source of the conflict, to raise us to a level of consciousness in which the conflict will be subdued, even overcome.

II Brown: *Life Against Death*

Brown's Freudian enterprise in *Life Against Death* to a remarkable extent mirrors that of Herbert Marcuse, the proverbial grandfatherly guru of the New Left. Marcuse's book *Eros and Civilization* was published in 1955 and Brown's *Life Against Death* was finished in 1956 though not published until 1959. I think it a stunning coincidence that two such different men, working from such different traditions, could parallel each other so closely in their respective diagnoses and cures for our communal ills. Marcuse, the German-atheist-Marxist-social philosopher, Brown the American-Oxfordian-Protestant-Classics scholar: both come to this point in their lives at a very similar juncture due to the deep claims that both staked in Freudianism. Later Marcuse retreats from his Freudian commitments back to a rather tepid liberal Marxism, and Brown later charges full forward to assume the role of almost religious visionary in *Love's Body*. So the two definitively part company during the sixties: but *Life Against Death* and *Eros and Civilization* play much the same tune to the fat and complacent Eisenhower fifties.

We can begin to pick out some themes in the tune if we compare the Brown of *Life Against Death* and the Marcuse of *Eros and Civilization* on the one hand, to Marx on the other.

Marx, despite the humanitarian sensitivity and the psychological insight which show up in the *Manuscripts of 1844*, was chiefly concerned throughout his lifetime with social oppression and with how to overcome it. Social oppression takes the form of class domination, that is the

exploitation of the working class by the ruling class.
The logic of domination is more complicated in modern industrial society than in this simple two class model, but in the end the result is always the same: the worker works, but he does not receive the full value out of his work, for that surplus value over and above his subsistence wages is raked off by the exploiters and thrown back into capital production and the management of the private property owned by the exploiting class. Consequently there is a kind of downward spiral of alienation from the products of their labor for members of the working class. The man who labors eight hours a day at the Ford Motor Company hardly feels a profound sense of accomplishment with the finished product, for he is responsible for only one tiny element in it, the same little element on an endless number of cars as they ceaselessly roll along the assembly line. So, at all events, the oppressors get richer, and the workers get poorer because the gap between them is constantly widening. Now the crucial note for our purposes in this line of Marxist thought is that the problem of oppression is formulated exclusively in economic terms. Accordingly the way out of oppression is also economic. A revolution of the proletariat working class would be effective only if it succeeded in overthrowing the dominance of the exploitative ruling class; in this situation private property would be abolished, the state would own the means of production, and the worker would be accorded the full value of his own labor. Only then, only after the success of the revolution, could the issue of humanitarian pursuits in the arts and other leisure activities arise, and Marx preferred to worry about that one after the revolution. The basic solution emphatically resides in the abolition of private property and ultimately even in the abolition of the state, for an egalitarian non-exploitative society could learn to subsist happily without the need for imposed authority: the workers would have lost their chains, and the state

would eventually wither away. These are the conditions upon which only could the individual live a non-repressed and therefore happy life.

Now Marcuse in *Eros and Civilization*, and Brown in *Life Against Death*, forge a radical departure from this account of things, although as I mentioned before, Marcuse has since retreated a good way back to it. The radical departure lies in the Freudian notion that the conditions of repression actually lie inside of us all. They are not merely functions of economic or social organization which would be excised by a different sort of socio-economic system.

Brown and Marcuse agree that cultural restraints, that is the way any society organizes itself and enforces its sanctions, values, and taboos, are inherently repressive for the individual. In other and simpler terms, nobody is able to do what he really wants to do because he must conform to the norms of his society. What we all really want to do in this context has to do with fulfilling our basic instinctual drives, primarily sexual ones. Notice that this is a very big claim indeed: we are unable to do what we really want to do, whether any of us realize that this is so or not. For, taking the cue from Freud, the argument goes that our basic drives are unconscious, inaccessible to our waking lives. So it is not only externally imposed customs and traditions, such as, for example, the work ethic in our society which repress us: rather repression begins before we are even aware that there are external restraints in the real world. This is to say that repression begins in infancy and becomes so much a part of us as time goes on that we are not even aware that we ourselves are putting down our basic instincts, making them do things other than what would happen if they were allowed free play. When an infant learns that he has to wait for the bottle or the breast, his basic drive for instant gratification is already waylaid. When he learns that he is supposed to use the toilet rather than urinate and defecate at will, he

once more finds himself deferring to authority and in fact
learning not to do precisely what he wants to do, which is
instantly to satisfy every bodily demand. In a nutshell:
as the infant learns to delay gratification, he is already
learning to repress himself: and eventually his image of
himself, of his own goodness, hinges on being able to repress himself and thus meet the expectations of others,
especially the parents during infancy.

To put all this in Freudian terms: at birth, infant
is wrenched from the cozy womb, where obviously no problem
arises about needs being instantly met. The infant at
this point is just a bundle of instinctual drives; he is
literally what Freud would call an It (*das Es*), an Id.
Only gradually does the infant learn to accept delayed
gratification and parental authority: gradually then what
Freud calls the ego (*das Ich*) grows from the bundle of
drives called the id, and gradually then a conflict grows
between ego and id: internalized ego essentially tells
id that it can't do what it wants to do, particularly at
this point because fear of punishment is strong enough to
waylay instinctual drives, but eventually because the
self-protective ego also resolves that it is *right* to restrain the id. That is, now things become a moral matter.
The child begins to impose restraints and limits *on himself* because it is *right* to do so and it would be *wrong*
not do so. That process of "moral" development represents
the growth of conscience (or superego), and any society
stands or falls on the degree to which it can successfully
instill a conscience in its children, a sense of right and
wrong, a willingness to obey the mores of the society,
and, at a gut level, to value for himself what the society
values for itself. Society, then, from infancy on, exacts
a price, and all of us pay the price in the degree to
which we repress ourselves.

Self-repression is also a process of self-forgetfulness. All those forbidden desires that we have for dependence and immediate sensual gratification are more and more forgotten, lodged in what Freud called the unconscious. And the traumas that we go through in infancy in order to achieve an acceptable level of self-repression are also forgotten, put away in the unconscious, there to stay so long as a strong ego can successfully keep them forgotten and inaccessible to conscious waking life (though of course they come out in dreams, fantasy, and slips of tongue). In a sense the ego knows those traumas are too painful to remember and therefore carefully constructs defenses against them--what Freud and later Anna Freud called defense mechanisms. Should, however, those memories also crop up in some neurotic symptom in later life, such as, for example, kleptomania, compulsive stealing, or again say in compulsive hand washing, or compulsive lying, or even depression, or whatever, we may have to come to terms with them all over again. To achieve successfully that painful reliving of the past is the aim of the therapeutic instrument developed by Freud called psychoanalysis.

Now let me summarize where we are: Brown and Marcuse, at least in the latter's book *Eros and Civilization*, buy this basic Freudian theory and in so doing they reject the Marxist idea that human nature is fundamentally free and perfectable, and that our unhappiness is solely due to social and economic oppression. Instead of Marx, Freud. All of us are involved in a severe inner conflict which I have here called self-repression and self-forgetfulness, and the more severely we repress ourselves, the higher the price we pay in guilt because it is extraordinarily difficult to put down and ignore the basic instinctual drives which provide the very energy for doing whatever we do. Channeling those drives into socially acceptable endeavors, such as, in our society, accumulating wealth and possessions, still leaves our instincts unsatisfied, because, at least for Freud, those instincts are of a primarily sexual nature. And as Freud said, money is not an infantile wish, so money in itself never is able to mitigate the primordial and incessant conflict between id and ego.

Now, with this background, let me concentrate for a

moment on Marcuse, so that perhaps you will see how much more seriously and farther Brown is willing to take this set of Freudian insights.

Marcuse admits that some form of societal organization is always necessary to overcome the problem of scarcity (*Anake*) and to control unrestrained behavior. But he thinks that societies have gone overboard, repressing the individual more than necessary, making him conform more than necessary according to the "performance principle" of any given society: this extra repression over and above the fundamentally necessary minimum repression is termed, imitating the Marxist surplus value concept, "surplus repression." To rid society, he thinks, of this extra repression would free the individual much more to indulge his drives and instincts: he would be free to play, to fantasize, to love, to create, in general to be exuberant and happy. This even more so, ideally, in modern mature industrial society because the problem of scarcity can be, Marcuse seemed to think, overcome on a worldwide scale. Basically, then, this proposal of Marcuse, if instantiated, would amount to an enormously reduced stock of guilt for the individual, obviously because there would be *fewer* norms to *fail to live up to*.

So far so good: but there is still a deeper problem, a malady that strikes at and cripples the individual man regardless of his social set-up and which cannot be eradicated by eradicating puritan repressive norms and capitalism. This is the repression inherent in *genital organization*. Marcuse recognizes genital organization as a problem, tries to resolve it in *Eros and Civilization*, but ultimately fails; and in fact in his later work he does not concern himself much with it, again concentrating his efforts at the social level, where once more reliant upon Marx, he worries about rearranging the structures of society so that they will become less exploitative, less repressive, and therefore less guilt producing.

In *Life Against Death*, however, Brown wants to deal

directly with and even solve this problem of genital organization. What, then, exactly is the problem? Freud located it in the crucial trauma of infancy, and gave that ordeal the name Oedipal Complex. Oedipus, as the Greek story has it, accidentally murdered his father and slept with his mother: for Freud these are precisely the two primal wishes shared by every individual in every society. All of mankind is characterized by them. Genital organization, or the focusing of sexual pleasure solely in the genital regions, comes about as a result of the thwarting of each child's desire to merge with the mother, literally, sexually, to get back inside the mother's body. Clearly to set the problem up this way goes beyond or behind social and cultural repressions. None of us, even in infancy, can have what he really wants.

But then, if the one most basic instinctual drive is to merge with the mother, and if total lack of repression is the goal, why not then simply do away with the incest taboo and allow mother-child sexual relations? Note that I am using the formulation mother-child since the same problem applies to both sons and daughters; infancy is androgynous or bisexual. The answer is that expunging the mother-child incest taboo would ignore the role of the father, who cannot allow his sexual role to be usurped by his children and therefore must impose his authority on his offspring. Father and child cannot compete for the same sexual object: this seems to be a biological given as incest taboos on mother-child sexual relations are universal so far as we know (although not at all on the relations father-daughter or brother-sister). Freud developed the elaborate myth of the primal horde, in which the brothers unite to kill the father and get the women, in order to account for the historical origins of paternal authority and the related mother-child incest taboo.

Now the point is that repression of the most basic drives that man has occurs on the most rudimentary level of societal organization, namely in the basic nuclear family situation, mother, father, infant. Here is where the real trouble starts, and even with a successful resolution of the Oedipal Complex by the child's acceptance of the father's authority and suppression of the dependent wish to merge with the mother, to get back into the womb, the child's drive to do so is not expelled and must be sublimated or rechanneled, mostly by some sort of achievements in the world (money, status, territorial wars, control over others, etc.). In disguised form, the primordial incestuous wish is also revealed in dreams and fantasy, in slips of the pen and tongue, and in personality traits in general. The initial Oedipal repression, furthermore, along with the guilt arising from continuing unconsciously to fantasize about having mother and killing father, leads to further repression, further acceptance of authority, and further guilt at being unable to fulfill perfectly all the norms that one is burdened with, especially as societies become more complex. A child's dependence on his parents gets translated more and more into dependent adult devotion to social and moral authority. Religion of course is involved here too: Freud argued that the ambivalent feelings which the child has toward the father--awe and hostility--are, in an unconscious attempt to resolve the ambivalence or conflict, projected onto a cosmic scale in the figure of God as supremely authoritative father image. I'll come back to the problem of religion later. For now the point is that Brown in *Life Against Death* wants to get to the unconscious root of the repression of the individual and find the way out from there--this is quite different, as you can see, from the Marxist utopian strategy. His elaborate diagnosis of genital organization as an acute malady and his recommendations for curing it also set Brown one removed from Marcuse.

A crucial and difficult point is that there is a connection between suppression of the drive to reunite with the mother and the eventual resolution of that drive by accepting the father's authority. That acceptance at puberty finally results in genital organization, concentration of sexual drives and energies and pleasures on the genital zones. Without the initial Oedipal repression, then, Brown argues that there would be no genital organization. I take this to mean that prior to genital organization, the entire body of the child is erotically charged, and that the form therefore of reunion with the mother is not just genital but total bodily pleasure. For this reason children may be said to have a richer sexual life than adults. "...various erotic activities, which are called perversions if they are pursued as substitutes for the normal sexual act, are called legitimate if they are subordinated as preliminaries to the normal sexual aim. Children, on the other hand, explore in indiscriminate and anarchistic fashion all the erotic potentialities of the human body. In Freudian terms, children are polymorphously perverse" (*Life Against Death*, p. 27).

When the possibility of the supreme pleasure of bodily reunion with the mother is obviated and repressed, then total bodily eroticism eventually recedes and locates in the genital region--this process is represented by the classical Freudian account of the process of reaching maturity, from the oral stage, through the anal, and finally to the phallic and after latency, the genital stage. The Oedipal conflict is settled at about age 5, then comes latency, then at puberty genital organization, the restrictive localization of erogenous pleasure. Human sexual development is therefore diphasic--there are two distinct stages of development separated by a period of latency from about 5 or 6 to 11 or 12. The second phase yields genital organization. Freud thought this process inevitable, the price of being human. Brown thinks that the process is inherently and wrongfully repressive, and that it can be overcome.

> We on the other hand cling to the position that Adam never really fell; that the children do not really inherit the sins of their fathers; that the primal crime is an infantile fantasy, created out of nothing by the infantile ego in order to sequester by

> repression its own unmanageable vitality (id); that the sexual organizations are constructed by the infantile ego to repress its bodily vitality; and that adult life remains fixated to this world of infantile fantasy until the adult ego is strong enough to enter the kingdom of enjoyment. "Atheism and a kind of second innocence complement and supplement each other," says Nietzsche. Only second innocence could recognize the whole debt and guilt complex as fantasy, as nightmare; only second innocence could be atheistical. Again we see the limitations of pseudosecular "rationalism." The ultimate problem is not guilt but the incapacity to live. The illusion of guilt is necessary for an animal that cannot enjoy life, in order to organize a life of non-enjoyment.
> (*Life Against Death*, p. 270)

Second innocence: we are not being instructed simply to *stay* at an infantile stage of development. Rather Brown is stating that it is necessary to go through the stage of genital organization, but then that it is possible to *reclaim* an infantile capacity for wholistic erogenous pleasure.

But how do we get ourselves round to really enjoying life in this way? Well, there's a two-sided answer to that question. Both sides begin on the individual level but then extend outward to have social consequences of the greatest imaginable magnitude. One side of the answer, the way out, lies in the concept *polymorphous perversity*; and the other side lies in the integration of death into life, so that life is not spent in the frantic avoidance of death by building up death-defying productions and achievements in the world. First of all, then, to be polymorphously perverse means to overcome genital organization, to revivify and resurrect the earliest infantile phase of life in which the entire body is erotically charged. Note again however that this is not a return to first or primal innocence. It is a second innocence, won as a result of reclamation of id territory. No longer then are basic instincts repressed; rather this repression is overcome; the energy of the id, expressed in libidinous or erotic drives, becomes free from dictatorial conscience. Freed from the authoritative and sadistic super-ego, the self can express heretofore suppressed urges openly, playfully, erotically. An "erotic sense of reality" would be created. All parts of the body will sensuously respond to the world and to others; sexual pleasure will no longer be confined to the genital organs.

Brown's conception of polymorphous perversity is the first of his answers to the problems of guilt and over-repression, or, if you will, the first of his recommendations about how to be happy rather than unhappy. The second of his solutions has to do with what he calls the integration of death into life. We are all in the business, he argues, of running frantically away from the death that ultimately looms before us. What Brown has in mind exactly on this point requires a bit of not uncomplicated explanation.

The key term which links genital organization with fear of death is sublimation; and sublimation is Brown's Freudian term for talking about our inability to live pleasurably instead of painfully. If you think of the id in Freudian terms as the source of all psychic energy, the locus of drives to do whatever we do at all, you must also think of it in conflict with the rational ego. The ego in a sense mediates between our bodies and external reality: it sorts stimuli out and lays instructions about what things to do on the id and the body. The ego always restricts the id by channeling its drives in only certain specified and socially acceptable directions. Laws, taboos, and etiquette are all involved. As the inner voice of authority, the conscience or super ego, grows, we all learn to regulate ourselves in acceptable ways without detailed directives from authorities such as parents or teachers. Conscience internalizes moral and behavioral demands, and, when we violate them, we pay a price in guilt. Think of the cost to a child when he is told by a parent that God is offended by his masturbating. It doesn't take long for that magisterial voice of God to get internalized. Further, since the instinctual drives lodged in the id are primarily sexual, the ego's voice is a moralizing one, a voice that restrains us from expressing ourselves sexually in the way that we really want to. As I said before, more and more of what we really want to do is repressed into the unconscious, so that we more and more are unable to remember what we really want to do. Only in earliest infancy are all those wants allowed free play, and none of us can remember what that was like--or, presumably, how nice it was.

On the other hand, this moralizing voice of the ego still has to deal with all these powerful, insistent id drives. It can't just say no; rather it has to redirect basic instinctual id drives into acceptable pursuits, which, in our society, are primarily non-sexual. Acceptable alternative pursuits are called sublimations by Freud. They do not represent what we really want to do, and in fact are decidedly second-best so far as our instincts are concerned. Once thwarted in our wish to merge back with mother, and once forced through fear to accept external authority, we are set into a process that mushrooms: we get set in the pattern of putting down our drives and we can indeed get fairly ferocious in our zeal for self-repression. We can and often do in fact positively lust after more and more sublimations, which are utterly unsatisfactory from the point of view of infantile desires for unrestrained expression of the id. Sublimations, such as work for instance, are only apparently satisfaction giving: in other words we fool ourselves into thinking that they satisfy us when actually they do not, though much of the time we are not consciously aware that this is the case. To put the argument in baldest terms: the fact that we fool ourselves into thinking that sublimations satisfy us, the fact that we aren't even aware of it, and the further fact that we are guilty when we indulge in real satisfaction-giving activities rather than the fake ones: all these are indications of our fundamental sickness. We are all, to one extent or another, very fundamentally neurotic. We repress ourselves, forget what we want, become guilty if we fail to repress ourselves further: as Brown incessantly points out, no other known animal would act in such a way. No other animal sublimates rather than living naturally. Man is the sole animal who is marked by his prediliction to make himself sick. Man is the neurotic animal, committed to setting up a life of non-enjoyment because he has forgotten how to enjoy himself naturally; the price he pays in guilt even for small pleasures is inordinate; and the rationales for why he is guilty, particularly religious ones, are phony. Guilt indicates a lack of self-tolerance and self-knowledge; and unrealistic hope for a dramatically better future is just the other side of the contemporary neurotic coin. Whether in the Marxist terrestrial version or the Christian celestial one, futural hope belies an inability genuinely to enjoy the present, and that, for Brown, is a hallmark of the self-duplicity which scars our truncated lives.

To be sure, death looms before us all. But Brown argues that if we were fully able to live a life of enjoyment, we would also be able without fear to face death as the fitting capstone for a fitting life. In our society, however, we try to run away from death by ignoring it--you know how the mass media extol the virtues of endless youth, and the cosmetics and fashion industries thrive. More important, we run away from death through the same process of sublimation that I have been mentioning: in our society the accumulation of wealth and possessions becomes almost an attempt to defy death: our suffocating immersion in material goods, our capitalistic stress on having and hoarding money for its own sake, our narcissistic and anxiety-ridden emphasis on our so-called achievements in the world--all these for Brown are ways in which we organize non-enjoyment and tell ourselves that it's all OK. And in all these ways we fail to integrate death into our lives because we are too fearful to do so, and that is the precise way of saying that we don't know how to live. We want estates to hand on rather than pleasurable lives. Not knowing how to live is epitomized by not knowing how to die. Brown quotes the poet Rilke: "Whoever rightly understands and celebrates death, at the same time magnifies life."

These are Brown's diagnoses in *Life Against Death*. His cure goes under the label of the resurrection of the body, a body relaxed, yet erotically charged in an infatile polymorphous perverse way; a body which *is* a soul, not different or divorced from the soul as some sham higher principle of life than the body; a body which does not work for the sake of work or accumulate money and possessions for the sake of money and possessions; a body which enjoys for the sake of enjoyment; a body unafraid of death because it is free of guilt for enjoying the present. As the Carly Simon song has it: these *are* the good old days. She like Brown is talking about a self that is not fixated on the past, nor unrealistic in the hope that somehow the future is going to be radically better than the present. Finally, a resurrected body is a body in which the conflict between id and ego is weighted toward id drives, toward the satisfaction of basic instinctual drives, in which, in other words, ego territory is reclaimed for id, and conscience ceases to make cowards of us all. The instinctual reality, as Brown says, is Dionysian drunkenness. To vivify some of this for you in Brown's own terms, I turn to some quotes from *Life Against Death*:

> Eternity is therefore a way of envisaging mankind's liberation from the neurotic obsession with the past and the future; it is a way of living in the present, but also a way of dying. Hence the ultimate defect of all heavens with immortality beyond the grave is that in them there is no death; by this token such visions betray their connection with repression of life. (p. 108)
>
> ...possessive mastery over nature and rigorously economical thinking are partial impulses in the human being (the human body) which in modern civilization have become tyrant organizers of the whole of human life; abstraction from the reality of the whole body and substitution of the abstracted impulse for

the whole reality are inherent in *Homo economicus*. In contrast, what would a nonmorbid science look like? It would presumably be erotic rather than (anal) sadistic in aim. Its aim would not be mastery over but union with nature. And its means would not be economizing but erotic exuberance. And finally, it would be based on the whole body and not just a part; that is to say, it would be based on the polymorphous perverse body. (p. 236)

And to miss the nature of the human disease is also to miss the nature of the cure. If the cause of the trouble were force, to "expropriate the expropriators" would be enough. But if force did not establish the domination of the master, then perhaps the slave is somehow in love with his own chains. If there is such a deeper psychological malady, then a deeper psychological regeneration is needed. (p. 242, [against Marx])

...for civilized man the crucial defense mechanism is sublimation. The basic characteristic of sublimation is the desexualization of sexual energy by its redirection toward new objects. But as we have seen, desexualization means disembodiment. New objects must substitute for the human body, and there is no sublimation without the projection of the human body into things; the dehumanization of man is his alienation of his own body. He thus acquires a soul (the higher spirituality of sublimation), but the soul is located in things. Money is "the world's soul." (p. 281)

This incapacity to die, ironically but inevitably, throws mankind out of the actuality of living, which for all normal animals is at the same time dying; the result is denial of life (repression). The incapacity to accept death turns the death instinct into its distinctively human and distinctively morbid form. The distraction of human life to the war against death, by the same inevitable irony, results in death's dominion over life. The war against death takes the form of a preoccupation with the past and the future, and the present tense, the tense of life, is lost--that present which Whitehead says "holds within itself the complete sum of existence, backwards and forwards, that whole amplitude of time, which is eternity." (p. 284)

Civilized man asserts his individuality, and makes history. But the individuality he asserts is not life-affirming or life-enjoying, but the life-negating (ascetic) individuality of (Faustian) discontent and guilt. Civilized individuality, in Nietzsche's image, does not want itself, but wants children, wants heirs, wants an estate. Life remains a war against death--civilized man, no more than archaic man, is not strong enough to die--and death is overcome by accumulating time-defying monuments. (p. 286)

The ever increasing denial of the body is, in the form of a negation, an ever increasing affirmation of the denied body. Sublimations are these negations of the body which simultaneously affirm it; and sublimations achieve this dialectical tour de force by the simple but basic mechanism of projecting the repressed body into things. The more the life of the body passes into things, the less life there is in the body and at the same time the increasing accumulation of things represents an ever fuller articulation of the lost life of the body. Hence increasing sublimation is a general law of history. Technological progress makes increased sublimation possible; and, as we argued in an earlier chapter, the hidden aim of technological progress is the discovery and recovery of the human body. (p. 297)

The withdrawal of Eros from sublimation is the great disillusionment. As modern civilization ruthlessly eliminates Eros from culture, modern science ruthlessly demythologizes our view of the world and of ourselves. In getting rid of our old loves, modern science serves both the reality-principle and the death instinct. Thus science and civilization combine to articulate the core of the human neurosis, man's incapacity to live in the body, which is also his incapacity to die. The human body had to be handed over to death before culture could produce psychoanalysis--the last assault on man's old loves and the first turn to face the body. (p. 303)

Psychoanalysis accepts the death of the body; but psychoanalysis has something to learn from body mysticism, occidental and oriental, over and above the wealth of psychoanalytical insights contained in it. For these mystics take seriously, and traditional psychoanalysis does not, the possibility of human perfectability and the hope of finding a way out of the human neurosis into that simple health that animals enjoy, but not man. (p. 311)

And that kind of perfectability is Brown's dream. Of course it is a utopian dream, but it is presented in realistic terms. It is based on Freud but not as such to be found in Freud, who had not a utopian bone in his body. Here Freud and Marcuse (of *Eros and Civilization*) are closer together than they are to Brown. Marcuse is really not too dissimilar from Brown up to this point, except for the crucial difference that he, like Freud, insists that not *all* repressions can be overcome or otherwise all organization would collapse. And gradually Marcuse takes this criticism of Brown's utopianism more and more seriously and begins to move back towards a more Marxist account of things. He too wants an eroticism to be infused into reality, but to do that reality itself must be changed. Nothing short of social and economic revolution can accomplish that. As Roszak points out, we get the same stoical renunciation ultimately from Marcuse that we get from Freud. Brown, I believe, stands out alone as the really radical utopian.

III Apocalypse:
The Place of Mystery in the Life of the Mind

But the shape of Brown's utopianism is nevertheless to alter drastically. He begins to abandon his demand for the social revolution which would be tied to the integration of the death instinct into life. His thought becomes more privatistic, so much so that it is even admitted to refer only to an elite, an elect fortunate enough to share in his vision. Quoting Pound, he states in "Apocalypse" that there are "...mysteries that cannot be revealed. Fools can only profane them" (p. 48). "Mysteries," he says,

> are unpublishable because only some can see them, not all.... Democratic resentment denies that there can be anything that can't be seen by everybody; in the democratic academy truth is subject to public verification; truth is what any fool can see. This is what is meant by the so-called scientific method: so-called science is the attempt to democratize knowledge--the attempt to substitute method for insight, mediocrity for genius, by getting a standard operating procedure. The great equalizers dispensed by the scientific method are the tools, those analytical tools. The miracle of genius is replaced by the standardized mechanism. But fools with tools are still fools, and don't let your Phi Beta Kappa key fool you. (p. 48)

Brown in "Apocalypse" begins to argue that we are in a time "when civilization has to be renewed by the discovery of new mysteries, by the undemocratic but sovereign power of the imagination, by the undemocratic power which makes poets the unacknowledged legislators of mankind, the power which makes all things new" (p. 48).

Despite the new departure indicated by these assertions, however, I think that Brown is still, in the "Apocalypse" oration, following up the groundwork laid in *Life Against Death*. And this long-term project can be characterized as an attempt to overcome the dualism about human nature so much a part of Western civilization from Plato to Descartes and Kant and the existentialists and the churches. "Breaking the boundaries" is the way Brown puts it. Dualism of mind and body, of nature and spirit, emotion and intellect, conscious and unconscious: these are pernicious and inherently repressive, especially at the expense of the body and bodily, erotic pleasures. The pleasures of the mind are asceptic, reified in books. Brown quotes Emerson: "the book becomes noxious: the guide is a tyrant. The sluggish and perverted mind of the multitude having once received this book, stands upon it, and makes an outcry if it is destroyed. Colleges are built upon it. Meek young men grow up in libraries. Hence instead of Man Thinking, we have the bookworm" (p. 49). Brown continues: "There is a hex on us, the specters in books, the authority of the past; and to exorcise these ghosts is the great work of magical self-liberation" (p. 49).

In the "Apocalypse" oration Brown really gets no further than simply extolling this magical self-liberation. "Apocalypse" is more a sermon than it is an argument. Still less is it a key that unlocks the door to unified, happy, erotically charged consciousness. Yet it is a most remarkable talk: imagine a professor of Classics giving a Phi Beta Kappa oration at Columbia University, in the heart of the Eastern intellectual establishment in this country; and the whole talk debunks reason, rationality, scientific method in favor of a kind of mad, irrational, Dionysian craziness. "Resisting madness can be the maddest way of being mad" (p. 47). Brown's kind of madness in "Apocalypse" just barely begins to adumbrate the final answer we get in *Love's Body*. "Apocalypse" essentially heaps praise on the imagination at the expense of logical, ordered reasoning. But *Love's Body* is not about the imagination; it is the fiery imagination in action; it is the work of the imaginative religious visionary, the seer. Some readers resonate to its message, some doubtless do not at all; for me personally, it called forth a response.

IV *Love's Body*

The following remarks present a chapter by chapter commentary on *Love's Body*, quoting passages from each chapter and then suggesting some brief thoughts on each. By way of introduction, I should like to refer to a conversation recorded by Carlos Castenada between himself and Don Juan, the Yanqui holy man. They have been tripping on what Don Juan calls Jimson Weed or the Devil's Weed. Carlos begins:

"Did I really fly, Don Juan?"

"That is what you told me. Didn't you?"

"I know, Don Juan. I mean, did my body fly? Did I take off like a bird?"

"You always ask questions I cannot answer. You flew. That is what the second portion of the devil's weed is for. As you take more of it, you will learn how to fly perfectly. It is not a simple matter. A man *flies* with the help of the second portion of the devil's weed. That is all I can tell you. What you want to know makes no sense. Birds fly like birds and a man who has taken the devil's weed flies as such."

"As birds do?"

"No, he flies as a man who has taken the weed."

"Then I didn't really fly, Don Juan. I flew in my imagination, in my mind alone. Where was my body?"

"In the bushes," he replied cuttingly, but immediately broke into laughter again. "The trouble with you is that you understand things only in one way" (*The Teachings of Don Juan* [Ballantine], pp. 130-31).

The trouble with you is that you understand things

in only one way. That's the basic message of *Love's Body* as well. Brown's indictment of us is that we understand things in only one way. We are literal minded.

I said earlier that Brown's overall project had to do with integration, with erasing pernicious dualisms, splits between mind and body, emotion and intellect, conscious and unconscious. But how to integrate mind and body? How to "get it together?" as we say in the contemporary idiom. How to overcome dualism? I suggest that Brown tries to forge a union through, not so much mysticism, as symbolism, especially body symbolism. Symbols link mind and body; symbols link a society to its view of what is transcendent, that which is ultimately important, one might say. And Brown learned from Freud that all symbolism basically stems from bodily and perhaps even erotic fantasies, dreams, projections. Thus with Ferenzci, one of Freud's early followers, Brown can say that there is a penis in every convex object, and a vagina in every concave one. There is no such thing as a mere object. It is always that *and* something else as well. All things mean more than one thing. All things are symbolic. Brown quotes from Blake: "Twofold always. May God us keep/From single vision and sleep" ("Apocalypse," p. 49). "Symbolism," says Robert Bellah, "is the link between conscious and unconscious, it is the way out of all dividing literalisms, it is the road to resurrection and reunion" (*Beyond Belief*, pp. 235-36).

The great religions find their places in this scheme of Brown's, not as great religious traditions, but as conveyors of great symbols which become forms for dealing with reality. Christian and Buddhist symbolism, psychoanalytic symbolism, mystical symbolism, symbolism from primitive traditions: all are available and relevant for Brown. *Religions* are repressive and alienating: but *religious symbolism* built on body symbolism is the way out for the individual, the way to overcoming fragmentation, literalism, loss of meaning and loss of enjoyment. In Theodore Roszak's words in *Making of a Counter Culture*, *Love's Body* is "the effort to recover from this pathological culture the traces of our disintegrated psychic wholeness and to fashion of these remnants a reality principle based on the organic unity which predated the advent of repression" (p. 115). Creating such a new reality principle is accomplished by living symbolically, through symbols that reflect all bodily instincts: symbol and body are one: both mean more than one thing: fragmentation is thus overcome and a new consciousness brought about. Brown, I think, is recommending that we live on this sort of level, not only to avoid dualism, but to avoid the almost infinite fragmentation and sense of chaos that living literally on only one level can bring, especially as that literalism is reinforced by equally fragmented and complex sets of social institutions.

With those preliminary remarks setting our conceptual framework, we may turn to the test, to our hermeneutical exercise, our effort to interpret and hence to learn. I begin by quoting from Chapter I, Liberty:

IV.1 Liberty

Freud's myth of the rebellion of the sons against the father in the primal, prehistoric horde is not a historical explanation of origins, but a suprahistorical archetype; eternally recurrent; a myth; an old, old story. (p. 3)

...taboos which prescribe sexual separation, mutual avoidance; the castration complex. Without an understanding of the seamy side of the sexuality there is no understanding of politics. (p. 11)

The ideology of utilitarianism which in the origin of the state and everywhere in life sees only obedience to necessity and the satisfaction of elementary vital needs, is senile, and in politics sees only senatorial activity. Youthful energy has that exuberance which overflows the confines of elementary necessity, and rises above labor into the higher, or is it lower, sphere of play. (p. 14)

Academic orthodoxy, senile and senatorial, is against fraternities; against Sparta; against Plato; against athletics; against play; against sex; against youth. (p. 14)

In the end, in accordance with the Freudian law of the return of the repressed, the murdered father returned and put an end to the quarreling of the brothers; it came to a choice between *libertas* and *pax*;... (p. 28)

Political parties are conspiracies to usurp the power of the father, "a taking of the sword out of the hand of the Sovereign." Political parties are antagonistic fraternities, or moieties;... (p. 29)

Behind liberty, freedom, our notion particularly of democratic freedom, there lies patricide, killing off the primal father or the king, and fratricide: Romulus and Remus, the myth which undergirded the dual organization of republican Rome. Just as the primal brothers need each other so we in our putative democracy need the warring party; every Nixon needs his Hiss, every Abbie Hoffman needs his Judge Julius Hoffman.

Behind the apparent rationality of the political process and behind what we think is freedom lies genital organization, the pair, male and female, warring even in coitus. Politics reflects dual organization which reflects genital organization: and in the game between the sexes, as in the game between the parties, all is power. The political analogue of polymorphous perversity is anarchy: breaking the boundaries of structured organization.

IV.2　Nature

"Maiden most beautiful, mother most beautiful, lady of lands, Queen and republican--"

She is our real mother:

"Hast thou known how I fashioned thee, Child, underground?" (p. 34)

Geography is the geography of the mother's body. (p. 36)

Already in childhood symbolic equivalents for the inside of the mother's body are discovered in external objects, the toys. Growing up consists in finding new toys, new symbolic equivalents; so that in all our explorations we are still exploring the inside of our mother's body. (p. 37)

The dance of life, the whole story of our wanderings; in a labyrinth of error, the labyrinth of this world. We wandering in the wilderness: Israel, Aeneas and his band of brothers to find Britain; the band of Pilgrims, compact together in one ship, to fly into the wilderness from the face of the dragon, from England to New England. The exodus is an initiation. (p. 40)

"Embryos we must be, till we burst the shell You ambient, azure shell, and spring to life." (p. 44)

The woman penetrated is a labyrinth. You emerge into another world inside the woman The penis is the bridge; the passage to another world is coitus; the other world is a womb-cave. Cave man still drags cave woman to his cave; all coitus is fornication (*fornix*, an underground arched vault). (p. 48)

The wandering heroes are phallic heroes, in a permanent state of erection; pricking o'er the plain. The word coition represents genital sexuality as walking; but the converse is also true: all walking, or wandering in the labyrinth, is genital-sexual. All movement is phallic, all intercourse sexual. Hermes, the phallus, is the god of roads, of doorways, of all goings-in and comings-out; all goings-on. (p. 50)

In the philosophy of Freud's *Beyond the Pleasure Principle* and Ferenczi's *Thalassa*, life itself is a catastrophe, or fall, or trauma. The form of the reproductive process repeats the trauma out of which life arose, and at the same time endeavors to undo it. The "uterine regressive trend in the sex act" is an aspect of the universal goal of all organic life--to return to lifeless condition out of which life arose. "The goal of all life is death." In this philosophy life and the main stages of biological evolution (sexual differentiation, adaptation to dry land) are catastrophes excited by external forces: these catastrophes create "tension"; and the aim of life (or of evolutionary adaptation) is to get rid of the tension, and so die. Life is a temporary (accidental) disturbance in a lifeless (and thus peaceful) universe. It is best, then, never to have been born; and second best, quickly to die. Nirvana is release from the cycle of rebirth. The real death is the death we are dead with here and now. (p. 53)

One of the themes in this chapter is the rejection of the sky god, the father figure magisterially running the universe. In place of the sky god we get the earth mother: or as for Black Elk, the Sioux medicine man: one walks on mother earth only in a sacred manner: each step on mother earth is sacred.

Another theme in Brown's chapter on Nature is movement, mobility. From ancestral home to the world outside. From the parents to college: *in loco parentis*: growing up absurd. Taking the burdens of our lives in our own hands--initiation into adult life: decisions, decisions: to cut ourselves off from the past and enter alone into the future. Jack Kerouac: On the Road; Ken Kesey: The Bus Trip--you're either on the bus or you're off the bus --electric kool-aid acid test.

Out of the cave and into the labyrinth: "This cave is grave: this womb is tomb." The analogue of the labyrinth of life is the vagina. The analogue of our movement is the penis. We go in and out of life: in and out: in and out: alternation of waking and sleeping.

The equation is: this life=slumber=death. We must wake up: we must be born again to the new life, the real life, of the resurrected body. Polymorphous perversity: symbolism: everything means more than one thing, "twofold always."

IV.3 Trinity

The parents in coitus make one flesh; not a juxtaposition of two separatenesses, but a genuine Two-in-One, incorporated; making one corporate body. "The father's penis incorporated in the mother"; "at this early stage of development the principle of *pars pro toto* holds good and the penis represents the father in person." (p. 60)

Mother and child as one body is mother with a penis. The symbolic equation, penis= child. The king entering the arch; the priest in the tent or tabernacle: "He is the Lamb and I the fold"; both a penis and a child. (p. 62)

In the ascent of the soul, the doffing of garments, the slipping of knots, the loosing of bonds, disaffiliation: "the sum of these knots is called 'psyche':--the complexes, or complications. (p. 74)

Zeus has an erection, in the head; and bears a child. And he bears a child via castration; his head is split by the blow of an axe. The father produces children from his head. Paternal power is not natural virility or paternity but castration denied; a lie, a veil made of the pubic hair of mother. "The father-image is a thin mask covering the image of the pre-Oedipal mother." "A great advance was made in civilization when men decided to put their inferences upon a level with the testimony of their sense and to make the step from matriarchy to patriarchy. The pre-historic figures which show a smaller person sitting upon the head of a larger one are representations of patrilineal descent; Athena had no mother, but sprang from the head of Zeus. A witness who testifies to something before a court of law is still called '*Zeuge*' [literally, 'begetter'] in German, after the part played by the male in the act of procreation; so too in hieroglyphics a 'witness' is represented pictorially by the male genitals." But the witness that stands up in the court is denying castration; the testimony is false testicles; and civilization a lie....

All work is woman's work. Every commodity is, as Marx says, a fetish, that is to say a non-existent penis. An investment. From feudal investiture to capitalistic investment, the manufacture of clothes for their own sake, not to be worn but to be saved in the hope chest. Instead of fixed robes and roles, fashion design and the endless search for identity: new personalities for old, turn in last year's model. The industrial revolution. Work is a masturbation dream, punishment for the Fall, which is falling asleep; and also a fall into division of the sexes. (pp. 77-78).

Trinity: the nuclear family: father, mother, child. All combined. Daddy's penis in mommy's hole: combined object, unity. The same as the child in the womb: penis and child both head for the womb, in and out, both in dream and in waking. In Christian symbolism, Father, Son, and Holy Spirit are all one being, one nature: trinitarian homogeneity or sameness, also the combined object.

This unity is the basic wish, the primal dream. But we do not fulfill its promises. We divide but do not conquer. We miss the connection, the coitus, between earth and sky, between self and others. We do not love. Instead we castrate ourselves, and not only our interminable work but also our sexual inversions are symptoms of our having only part rather than the whole--sado-mashochism, transvestitism, onanism, homosexuality--all are attempts to regain the primordial unity of the combined object. The female with a penis is the symbol of what we so dearly wish: it is the ultimate symbol of unity that has cropped up in remarkably diverse cultural settings. The symbol of the female with a penis is the ultimate symbol of trinitarian unity, father, mother, and child all in one.

IV.4 Unity

Is there a way out; an end to analysis; a cure; is there such a thing as health?

To heal is to make whole, as in wholesome; to make one again; to unify or reunify: this is Eros in action. Eros is the instinct that makes for union, or unification, and Thanatos, the death instinct, is the instinct that makes for separation, or division. (p. 80)

Crazy Jane in William Butler Yeats--Crazy Jane who is both the student and the teacher--says,

> Nothing can be sole or whole
> That has not been rent.

We have been rent; there is no health in us. We must acknowledge the rents, the tears, the splits, the divisions; and then we can pray, as Freud prays at the end of *Civilization and Its Discontents*, "that the other of the two heavenly forces, eternal Eros, will put forth his strength so as to maintain himself alongside his equally immortal adversary." (pp. 80-81)

The unification of the human race: a mental fight, a struggle in and about men's minds. The rents, the tears, splits and visions are mindmade: they are not based on truth but on what the Buddhists call illusion, what Freud calls unconscious fantasies. The prevailing sense of reality, the prevailing forms of knowledge, are fueled by the instinct of aggression and vision, are under the dominion of the death instinct. We are in Satan's kingdom; to build a Heaven in Hell's despite is to construct an erotic sense of reality.

To make in ourselves a new consciousness, an erotic sense of reality, is to become conscious of symbolism. Symbolism is mind making connections (correspondences) rather than distinctions (separations). Symbolism makes conscious interconnections and unions that were unconscious and repressed. (pp. 81-82)

Union and unification is of bodies, not souls. The erotic sense of reality unmasks the soul, the personality, the ego; because soul, personality and ego are what distinguish and separate us; they make us individuals, arrived at by dividing till you can divide no more--atoms.... Souls, personalities, and egos are masks, spectres, concealing our unity as body. For it is as one biological species that mankind is one--"the species-essence" that Karl Marx looked for; so that to become conscious of ourselves as body is to become conscious of mankind as one. (p. 82)

If we are all members of one body, then in that one body there is neither male nor female; or rather there is both: it is an androgynous or hermaphroditic body, containing both sexes.... The division of the one man into two sexes is part of the fall; sexes are sections. (p. 84)

In the collective unconscious Freud finds what he calls an "archaic heritage," or "phylogenetic inheritance." "Phylogenetic inheritance," i.e., belonging to the "species-essence" of the human species. "Archaic heritage," i.e., archetypes; at any rate the phylogenetic factor is the symbolic factor, the former identity or lost unity which symbolic consciousness recovers. "There probably exists in the mental life of the individual not only what he has experienced himself, but also what he brought with him at birth, fragments of a phylogenetic origin, an archaic heritage." Not in entire forgetfulness do we come. Freud comes to the conclusion that "the archaic heritage of mankind includes not only dispositions, but also ideational contents, memory traces of the experiences of former generations." The nucleus of neurosis turns out to be precisely in this phylogenetic factor: not in the individual's own murderous impulses against his individual father, but in the primal crime against the primal parent or parents. For Freud, then, in the end, as for Christianity, in Adam's fall we sinned all, and there is just that one collective sickness of the human race in all its generations: we are all in the same boat, or body. (pp. 87-88)

The *id* is instinct; that Dionysian "cauldron of seething excitement," a sea of energy out of which the ego emerges like an island.... The reality is instinct, and instinct is impersonal energy, an "it" who lives in us. I live, yet not I, but it lives in me; as in creation, *fiat*. Let it be; no "I," but an it. (p. 88)

Once we are cursed with body-soul dualism, there can be no unity, no unification, no triumph of Eros. Unification of mankind, if it is to be, is biological, and biological is anatomical, and anatomical is the body. Unification has to do with bodies not souls, and with ids not egos. The unified body of mankind is androgynous, hermaphroditic, bisexual, neither male nor female, the combined subject. The "mystical or symbolical body." Utopian. But as Brown says in *Life Against Death*, even the very survival of humanity today is a utopian hope.

IV.5 Person

Fixed personalities; unchanging masks; character is carving. When Marcus Aurelius says, "carve your mask," he means "develop your character." Stereotypes. All personality is rigid--"This is the way to do things, and this is the only way"--magical, and mechanical; a mechanization of a particular way of reacting; a repetition-compulsion. (p. 95)

A person is always a feigned or artificial person, *persona ficta*. A person is never himself, but always a mask; a person never owns his own person, but always represents another, by whom he is possessed. And the other that one is, is always ancestors; one's soul is not one's own, but daddy's. This is the meaning of the Oedipus Complex. (p. 98)

Instead of the cyclic recurrence of a temporary role, the historical personage offers a continuous performance and achieves a continuous existence. (p. 100)

The ego is public relations. (p. 101)

Patrilineal inheritance is not for the sake of the sons, but for the sake of the defunct father. (p. 102)

The construction of the super-ego moves the open-air theater indoors. (p. 103)

Freud says that the condition for giving up an external love-object is to make out of oneself a substitute for the lost object; part of the ego dresses up as father and says to the id, "Look, I am so like father, you can just as well love me instead." So Roheim can say, "By personality we mean that each individual grows up by wearing a mask, by imitating one of his parents." (p. 104)

God does not go for personalities; nor does the Last Judgment consist in the award of prizes to personalities for the performance of their parts. The performance principle must go; the show must not go on. (p. 105)

Again there are some important themes which appear in this chapter, and some old themes recur in new form. Like an orchestral score, themes appear, are transformed, and disappear only to appear again in a new context. The argument of *Love's Body* does not move according to the pattern of Aristotelian logic: premise, premise, premise, deduction. Rather it moves in spiral fashion, round and round, until its points are nailed home, and we see, we have insight: not just intellectual conviction but genuine insight.

The master theme in the Person chapter is that life in the modern world is unselfconscious masquerade; we all play roles all the time and the unfortunate thing is that we are not, like the primitive, aware that all those things we do, all those interpersonal relationships, are theatrical roles, masquerades. We Puritans take those roles seriously, victims as we are of the performance principle.

Brown pins this indictment on modern Western man via a historical analysis--the development of individualism in Greece is the root of the modern form of egoistic slavery to the performance principle. Shape up or ship out: we must perform, we must make it; others must think well of us; after all, they have expectations which we are supposed to meet. In modern non-cyclical or linear history, we children incarnate our fathers, and their expectations must be attended to: are we not to make up for *their* shortcomings and thus keep *their performances* going? How else can they escape from death unless their immortality is guaranteed by the deeds of the sons? The fathers reincarnate themselves in the sons via conscience, superego. Conscience or superego is the internalized voice of the father living on in perpetuity: it is the watchful voice inside me, the voice of authority, the prohibiting voice, telling me what I cannot do. Conscience doth make cowards of us all.

We are all involved in this same public show, this same vast theatre of the absurd. And we are all so vain:

we all do think that this song is about us. We are egomaniacal: we engage in frenetic performance for the sake of approbation, never thinking that inactivity might be a far richer and more fruitful life project than hurly burly activity designed to convince others of our worth and designed also to convince ourselves of our own worth.

The Big Father, God the all seeing, must die for the show not to go on. Otherwise we, the children, are doomed to the endless theatrical performances: but all the world's a stage only if we thoughtlessly and self repressively continue to make it so.

IV.6 Representative

...the Couretes, the young men of the war dance, have a Leading Man. More and more they differentiate him from themselves, make him their vicar. Their attitude becomes more and more one of contemplation. More and more they become spectators, of his action. Theatrically speaking, they become an audience; religious speaking, they become worshippers; he becomes a god. Gradually they lose all sense that the god is themselves. "He is utterly projected." (p. 117)

It is a mental alienation; a permanent reduction of the self to a condition of tutelage, as in minors or madmen. (p. 117)

Vicarious satisfaction: the deed is both theirs and not theirs. On this self-contradiction, this hypocrisy, this illusion, representative institutions are based.
   In vicarious experience there is both identification and distance. The mediator is to keep reality at a distance, to keep the multitude in remote contact with reality. Hobbes saw the paradigm in Exodus XX, 18-19: "And all the people saw the thundering, and the lightnings, and the noise of the trumpet, and the mountain smoking; and when they saw it, they removed, and stood far off. And they said unto Moses, Speak thou with us, and we will hear: but let not God speak with us, lest we die." Representative institutions depend upon the distance separating the spectators from the actor on the stage; the distance which permits both identification and detachment; which makes for a participation without action; which establishes the detached observer, whose participation consists in seeing and is restricted to seeing; whose body is restricted to the eyes. Everything which is merely seen is seen through a windowpane, distantly; and purely: a pure aesthetic experience. Representative institutions depend upon the aesthetic illusion of distance. (pp. 119-20)

The garden is polymorphism of the senses, polymorphous perversity, active interplay; and the opposite of polymorphous perversity is the abstraction of the visual, obtained by putting to sleep the rest of the life of the body. (p. 121)

The penis which still belongs to another;
even as our superego still belongs to Daddy.
The super-ego is borrowed strength; or a
stolen trophy; a head cut off, a monument
erected high in our house. To idealize is
to idolize; to make an idol; to translate
into a fixed image for contemplation; to
turn into monumental form; to turn into
stone. To concentrate on seeing is to turn
into stone; Medusa's head; castration. (p. 124)

Politically we are endlessly docile. We lust after authority. Toward authority we are infantile-dependent. We foist off our responsibility on others: our vicars act vicariously in our places. So we become detached observers, and the presidency can be turned into a virtual dictatorship just under our lethargic gazes. The parallel is with a child's-eye view of the primal scene, the parents in coitus: and "the effect," as Brown says, "of the primal scene is castration." We become voyeurs rather than participators. Genital organization rather than polymorphous perversity.

IV.7 Head

The apocalypse lays bare the mystery of kingship; stripping off the Emperor's New Clothes, to reveal the harlot. Kingship is fornication--the identity of politics and sex. In the apocalypse the walls do fall; the walls separating inside and outside; public and private; body physical and metaphysical. The identification of sex and politics; as in psychoanalysis. (p. 126)

Psychoanalysis shows the sexual organization of the body physical to be a political organization; the body is a body politic. Psychoanalysis stands or falls on the expansion of the idea of sexuality to comprehend the entire life of the human body; attributing a sexual ("erotogenic") action to all parts, organs, or "zones"; or rather, envisaging sexuality as an energy diffused throughout the whole body, and capable of displacement from one part to another, and of transformation from one mode of manifestation to another (polymorphism; metamorphosis). What the psychoanalytically uninitiated call "sex," psychoanalysis calls "genitality," or "genital organization," seeing in it an arrangement, a *modus vivendi*, a political arrangement arrived at after stormy upheavals in the house of Oedipus. The arrangement is to concentrate sexuality in one part of the body, the genital; this concentration, or organization, establishes the "primacy" of one "component-impulse," which is now the "dominating" or "supreme" component-impulse in the sexual life of the body. It is, says Freud, a well-organized tyranny of a part over the whole. (pp. 126-7)

It is part of the tyranny of genital organization that its slaves are blind, and see not tyranny but natural necessity. The status quo bears the seal of familiarity, until the seal is broken; the apocalypse. The revolutionary idea in psychoanalysis is the idea of the body as a (political) organization, a body politic; as a historical variable; as plastic. Man Makes Himself, his own body; his image of the body; the Eternal Body of Man is the Imagination. (p. 127)

The body, like the body politic, is a theater, everything is symbolic, everything including the sexual act. The principal part is a public person taking the part of the community as a whole: *persona publica totius communitatis gerens vicem*. The function of the representative organ is to impersonate, incarnate, incorporate in his own body the body politic. Incorporation is the establishment of a theater (public); the body of spectators depend on the performance for their existence as one body. (pp. 131-32)

The penis is the head of the body, the band of brothers; the rest of the body is to the penis as chorus to tragic hero, hypocritically and from a safe distance enjoying the thrill of being spectators at their own execution. (p. 132)

The head, the husband, and the soul of the body. The classic psychoanalytical equation, head=genital. Displacement is not simply from below upwards; nor does the truth lie in simply reducing it all downwards (psychoanalytical reductionism). The way up is the way down; what psychoanalysis has discovered is that there is both a genitalization of the head and a cerebralization of the genital. The shape of the physical body is a mystery, the inner dynamical shape, the real centers of energy and their interrelation; the mystical body which is not to be arrived at by anatomical dissection and mechanical analysis; the symbolical life of the body, with which psychoanalysis can put us in touch. (p. 136)

To talk about polymorphous perversity is to talk about the imagination. To reeroticize the body we must also reeroticize the head. To overcome genital organization is to overcome body-soul dualism is to overcome the tyrannical domination of one part of the body over the others, and finally, to overcome genital organization is to overcome egoism. Politics and genitality: the president and the prick: that we allow both to play leading roles is part of our theatrical self-repression and self-forgetfulness. Sex and politics: both the theatre of the poor said Talleyrand. Amidst riches we are poor, precisely because we have made fetishes of our commodities and emptied or ejaculated ourselves into them. Psychic and symbolic deprivation: "Workers of the world, unite! Throw off your chains," said Marx: but Freud said that would be hard to do because we are in love with our own chains.

IV.8 Boundary

The possibilities adumbrated in infancy are to be taken as normative: as in Wordsworth's "Ode": "before shades of the prison house close in; before we shrink up into the fallen condition which is normal adulthood." (p. 141)

"The ambitions of the Id, while that was the sole governing force, were towards *being* the thing at the other side of whatever relationship it established. When the Ego takes control of the Id's impulses, it directs them towards *having*." (p. 145)

"The natural man is self-centered, or ego-centric; everything he regards as real he also regards as outside himself; everything he takes 'in' immediately becomes unreal and 'spectral.' He tries to become an armored crustacean alert for attack or defense; the price of selfishness is eternal vigilance. This kind of Argus-eyed tenseness proceeds from the sealed prison of consciousness which Blake calls 'opaque.'" (p. 148)

Separateness, then, is the fall—the fall into division, the original lie. Separation is secrecy, hiding from one another, the private parts or property. Ownership is hiding; separation is repression. It is a private corporation. (pp. 148-49)

There is, then, after all a sense in which the body is not real; but the body that is not real is the false body of the separate self, the reality-ego. That false body we must cast off; in order to begin the Odyssey of consciousness in quest of its own true body. (p. 154)

Reality is not things (dead matter, or heavy stuff), in simple location. Reality is energy, or instinct; (p. 155)

To overcome dualism would be to awake out of sleep; to arise from the dead. (p. 159)

Definitions are boundaries; schizophrenics pass beyond the reality-principle into a world of symbolic connections: "all things lost their definite boundaries, became iridescent with many-colored significances." Schizophrenics pass beyond ordinary language (the language of the reality-principle) into a truer more symbolic language: (p. 160)

   The mad truth: the boundary between sanity and insanity is a false one. The proper outcome of psychoanalysis is the abolition of the boundary, the healing of the split, the integration of the human race. (p. 160)

Possessions establish boundary lines between what is mine and what is yours. I am what I own, my private parts. If I empty myself out into the things which I possess, then I no longer have an inner reality: that is to say, everything that is real to me comes to exist out there, outside of me. I have projected reality there and thus made it real. "Out there" is the domain of the reality principle: the things we have made or projected or possessed actually possess and control us. We must reclaim inner reality by breaking down the pernicious boundaries between inner and outer and between thee and me. We must learn to love, to experience and live the power of Eros to unite rather than divide; we must energize or eroticize that which is real. Otherwise we are only talking about inert, dead things. It is not dead matter that really matters. Not to be mad may indeed be the maddest sort of madness. Captain Ahab: madness maddened. As Ronald Laing insists, schizophrenics have a hold on reality and truth that non-schizophrenics do not. The mad, Dionysian truth.

IV.9 Food

Eating is the form of redemption. Except ye eat the flesh of the Son of man, and drink his blood, ye have no life in you. We must eat again of the tree of knowledge, in order to fall into innocence. (p. 167)

Transubstantiation--the whole problem of symbolism. Metaphor is really metamorphosis: (p. 168)

From the bloody to the bloodless sacrifice: from the literal to the spiritual body. Real presence, in a bloodless sacrifice; not sublimation, but transubstantiation of the body. (p. 173)

Brown's chapter on food obviously utilizes Christian symbolism as its most central structural theme. "Take and eat, for this is my body." Christian eucharistic symbolism. Cannibalism. Eating the son to incorporate the father: again the building up of internal super ego or conscience and the growth of guilt. And of course Brown the Freudian is never far from the sexual undertones of all symbolism, for all symbolism is ultimately based in the body. Thus the equation also is: eating=communion= oral copulation. "They are nourished by one another," he says. And when Brown talks about self sacrifice in this chapter, I think he is again striking the theme of learning to love by giving oneself. Separation gives way to unity. Nothing can be whole that has not first been rent, rent away from egoistic hoarding and thrown toward communal sharing.

IV.10 Fire

The choice is between partial incorporation and total incorporation (integration). Participation (playing a part) of fusion. Total incorporation, or fusion, is combustion in fire. (p. 176)

The true sacrifice is total, holocaust. *Consummatum est.* The one is united with the all, in a consuming fire. (p. 177)

Love is all fire; and so heaven and hell are the same place. As in Augustine, the torments of the damned are part of the felicity of the redeemed. Two cities; which are one city. Eden is a fiery city; just like hell. (p. 179)

Find the true fire; of which the fires of war are a Satanic parody. Fight fire with fire. The true teachers of peace are those who have the highest power, who can work miracles, who are masters of fire. Therefore the Buddhas are called Jinas, Conquerors. (p. 181)

The thing, then, is not to abolish war but to find the true war. Open the hidden Heart in Wars of Mutual Benevolence, Wars of Love. (p. 182)

Save us from the literal fire. The literal-minded, the idolaters, receive the literal fire. Each man suffers his own fire. (p. 182)

The real fire, the chariot of fire, the Fiery Chariot of his Contemplative Thought. The real fight, the mental fight; poetry, a sword of lightning, ever unsheathed, that consumes the scabbard that would contain it. (p. 183)

In this chapter Brown contrasts literal fire with the fiery imagination, the transcendent power of the embodied mind. Not mind as the mundane computer-like storehouse of information, but the visionary, mystical, imaginative capacities of mind. Fire is the symbol of the Apocalypse, of the apocalyptic reversal that, for Brown, must occur for mankind to survive. Fire is an answer to the question of whether we shall make it. Error is literalism and idolatry: it must be consumed as in a holocaust: only then can truth emerge, the truth of symbolical consciousness, the new and for the first time enduring head trip. Purification of the head by fiery purge of literalism and egoism and thus a liberation of the embodied mind.

IV.11 Fraction

There is a seal or sepulcher to be broken, a rock to be broke open, to disclose the living water; an eruption. Begin then with a fracture, a cesura, a rent; opening a crack in this fallen world, a shaft of light. (p. 185)

Literal meanings are icons become stone idols; the stone sepulcher, the stone tables of the law. (p. 185)

The crucified body, the crucified mind. The norm is not normality but schizophrenia, the split, broken, crucified mind. (p. 186)

Exaggeration or extravagance; not to count the cost. Go for broke. Aphorism is recklessness; it goes too far. Intellect is courage; the courage to risk its own life; to play with madness. (p. 187)

Symbolism, or grotesque: "A fine grotesque is the expression, in a moment, by a series of symbols thrown together in bold and fearless connection, of truths which it would have taken a long time to express in any verbal way, and of which the connection is left for the beholder to work out for himself; the gaps, left or overleapt by the haste of the imagination, forming the grotesque character." (pp. 188-89)

Broken speech; speech broken by silence. To let the silence in is symbolism. "In symbol there is concealment and yet revelation: here therefore, by Silence and by Speech acting together, comes a double significance." (p. 190)

Brown is beginning, as you must notice, in these last chapters to build in intensity, almost as if he were performing an act of intercourse with our minds which will erupt and end in Nothing (ch. 16), peace, nirvana. I can simply list the barely mentioned primary ideas of the fraction chapter. In it there is an important defense of the aphoristic style that characterizes the whole of *Love's Body*: the aphorism as opposed to the system of thought: magical, intuitive insight as opposed to thought packaged and bound by Aristotelian logic. Only with the aphorism can there be both speech and silence, the said and the not said. The system tries to say it all, which is why all systems of thought are unsuccessful, one-sided, fragmentary, and oh so serious. The aphorism is open ended and lively and playful: the aphorism allows for both speech and silence at the same time, and thus we readers can fill in the gaps for ourselves. Aphorism, following McLuhan, is a cool medium; the system is hot. Really to read Brown, then, is to participate in Brown's thought: *Love's Body* cannot genuinely be read from the point of view of the detached observer. It must engage us so that we fill in our own gaps; otherwise, it too fails.

To mention other primary themes in Fraction: breakthrough: grotesque: exaggeration: intellectual courage: courageous intellect: thought=semen=life: painful rebirth through brokenness, which of course expresses the mysterious old paradox: only he who loses himself can find himself. There is a rock to be broken; go for broke.

IV.12 Resurrection

Literal meanings as against spiritual or symbolical interpretations, a matter of Life against Death. The return of symbolism, the rediscovery that everything is symbolic. (p. 191)

The return to symbolism would be the end of the Protestant era, the end of Protestant literalism. (p. 191)

So also the psychoanalytic principle of over-determination: "Psychical acts and structures are invariably over-determined." The principle of over-determination declares that there cannot be just one "true" interpretation of a symptom or symbol: it forbids literal-mindedness. (p. 193)

The book is a materialization of the spirit; instead of the living spirit, the worship of a new material idol, the book. (p. 195)

There is another kind of Protestantism possible; a Dionysian Christianity; in which the scripture is a dead letter to be made alive by spiritual (symbolical) interpretations; in which meaning is not fixed, but ever new and ever changing; in a continuous revelation; by fresh outpouring of the holy spirit. Meaning is made in a meeting between the holy spirit buried in the Christian and the holy spirit buried underneath the letter of scripture; a breakthrough, from the *Abgrund*, from the unconscious of the reader past the conscious intention of the author to the unconscious meaning; breaking the barrier of the ego and the barrier of the book. (p. 196)

Redemption is symbolism. (p. 202)

The spirit is understood by the spirit; by the same spirit, i.e., in the same style. The proper response to poetry is not criticism but poetry. (p. 205)

The dead letter. The dead metaphor. It is only dead metaphors that are taken literally, that take us in (the black magic). Language is always an old testament, to be made new; rules, to be broken; dead metaphor, to be made alive; literal meaning, to be made

symbolical, oldness of letter to be made new
by the spirit. (p. 207)

Literalism, and futurism, are to distract us
from the reality of the present. (p. 207)

We must rise from history to mystery: (p. 214)

    To rise from history to mystery is to
experience the resurrection of the body here
now, as an eternal reality; to experience
the *parousia*, the presence in the present,
which is the spirit; to experience the re-
incarnation of the incarnation, the second
coming; which is his coming in us. (p. 214)

This chapter is perhaps the most thoroughly Christian one in *Love's Body*. But of course Brown is using Christian symbolism to do in Christianity as an institutional religion based on a once and for all historical event which purportedly happened some two thousand years ago. Unless you have had some training in the literature of Christianity they are hard to spot, but some brilliant vignettes are offered by Brown in this chapter, some scathingly finding the soft underbelly of modern Christian theology and biblical scholarship.

The major emphases that Brown is insisting upon in the Resurrection chapter seem to me these: first an exhortation to break out of the bonds that hold us to linear historical time, as if we thought the historical process were really getting us somewhere. Brown again opts for the image of cyclical time. Things recur, they do not happen once and for all. To think that time only moves in a linear, one-way fashion is to become enslaved to the literal historical. To move beyond that is to move beyond the letter to the spirit. Brown is arguing against Protestant fundamentalism, against Roman Catholic scholastic literalism, and against academic orthodoxy with its dead pseudo-commitment to the books. All this barrage is aimed, it seems to me, at healing the breach between religion and science, for one thing, and at healing as well the breach between the soft hearts of the humanists and the hard heads of the experimental researchers.

For us ever to worry about "how it really happened" is to involve ourselves in the mechanical literalism that Brown indicts in the modern university, the same phenomenon that Bellah calls "establishment fundamentalism." But to get off being hooked on "how it really happened" is to read history as poetry. Of course that also means that the proper response to history is poetry: not the academic historical-critical approach to a dead thing, but a playful, open-ended, poetic, symbolic, polymorphous approach to all that is about us in the present. Again, Carly Simon: These *are* the good old days.

IV.13 Fulfillment

God being thus hidden, every religion which does not affirm that God is hidden, is not true; and every religion which does not give the reason of it, is not instructive. Psychoanalysis passes the test. (p. 216)

Symbolic consciousness is between seeing and not seeing. It does not see self-evident truths of natural reason; or visible saints. It does not distinguish the wheat from the tares; and therefore must as Roger Williams saw, practice toleration; or forgiveness, for we never know what we do. The basis of freedom is recognition of the unconscious; the invisible dimension; the not yet realized; leaving a space for the new. (p. 217)

The unconscious to be made conscious; a secret disclosed; a veil to be rent a seal to be broke open; the seal which Freud called repression. Not a gradual process, but a sudden breakthrough. A reversal of meaning; the symbolism suddenly understood. The key to the cipher: the sudden sight of the real Israel, the true bread, the real lamb. (p. 217)

Symbolical consciousness—Christian, or psychoanalytical, or Dionysian—terminates in the body, remains faithful to the earth. The dreamer awakes not from a body but to a body. Not an ascent from body to spirit, but the descent of spirit into body: incarnation not sublimation. (pp. 221-22)

Literalism makes the world of abstract materialism; of dead matter; of the human body as dead matter. Literalism kills everything, including the human body. (p. 223)

Literalism makes a universe of stone, and men astonished, petrified. Literalism is the ministration of death, written and engraven in stones; tables of stone and stony heart. (p. 223)

To return the word to the flesh. To make knowledge carnal again; not by deduction, but immediate by perception or sense at once; the bodily senses. (p. 224)

Life is the power to make new life; the spirit is phallic, and fiery; the god is Dionysian. (p. 224)

To reconcile body and spirit would be to recover the breath-soul which is the life-soul instead of the ghost-soul or shadow; breath-consciousness instead of head-consciousness; body-consciousness instead of head-consciousness. The word made flesh is a living word, not a scripture but a breathing. A line that comes from the breath, from the heart by way of the breath. Aphorism as utterance: a short breath, drawn in pain. Winged words, birds released from the sentence, doves of the spirit. (p. 213)

Brown argues that if we consider life to be a sort of dream then we can interpret and understand it as we do a dream, which is to say polymorphously; for everything in a dream means a multitude of things, never just one thing. Thus, everything that is and everything that happens is *overdetermined* in meaning; again which is to say that nothing means only one thing.

Shadow is to sublimation as light or dawn is to the body. To sublimate is to turn away from the reality of the body to shadowy realities like the commodities devotedly extolled to us over the TV. Again here Christian symbolism is central; Christ is the Word made flesh, adumbrating the fulfillment of the final turn to the symbolic body (the bodily symbol) and away from the darkness of literalism and repressive sublimation.

IV.14 Judgment

Symbolic consciousness, a trance, in transit: going over, from this world to the next. Overcoming this world. (p. 233)

From this world to the next; from utility to creation. Instead of words as market-place utilities, brand names to advertise established items, the creative words which make it new. Words made new again, as on the first day of creation; eternity's sunrise. Words used not to interpret the world but to change it; not to advertise this world but to find another. To pass from this world to the next; from ordinary to extraordinary language. (p. 234)

Overthrow the reality-principle: no respect for persons, not to be fooled by masks; no clothes, no emperor. All power is an impostor; a paper tiger, or idol; it is Burnt up the Moment Men cease to behold it. The Last Judgment is the Vision; the political act is the poetical act, the creative vision. (p. 235)

Psychoanalysis is that revolving stage which completes this revolution, disclosing the bedroom and the bathroom behind the bourgeois facade, disclosing the obscenity of the onstage scene, abolishing the reality-principle and its unreal distinction between public and private, between head and genital. (p. 236)

Everything is symbolic, everything is holy. There is no special time or place or person, privileged to represent the rest. And then democracy can begin. The many are made one when the totality is in every part. When one thing is taken up, all things are taken up with it; one flower is the spring. It is all there all the time. (p. 239)

Upside down. Not the reality-principle but surrealism. Surrealism, a systematic illumination of the hidden places and a progressive darkening of the rest; a perpetual promenade right in the forbidden zone. (p. 241)

Politics dissolves into poetics if we alter our vision and our consciousness. Political power is powerful only if we are respecters of it. All of us, not just our so-called leaders, are the grains of sand which are infinity.

Symbolical consciousness overcomes the distinction between sacred and profane, and between master and slave. "Freud's discovery: the universal underworld." But that underworld of Freud's means that things are not what they seem, that things actually are upside down, and perhaps we can "seduce the world to madness" after all.

IV.15 Freedom

Freedom is poetry, taking liberties with words, breaking the rules of normal speech, violating common sense. Freedom is violence. (p. 244)

The original sense is nonsense; and common sense a cover-up job, repression. Psychoanalysis, symbolic consciousness, leads from disguised to patent nonsenses--Wittgenstein, surrealism, *Finnegan's Wake*. (p. 245)

No things, but an iridescence in the void. Meaning is a continuous creation, out of nothing and returning to nothingness. If it is not evanescent it is not alive. Everything is symbolic, is transitory; is unstable. The consolidation of meaning makes idols; established meanings have turned to stone. (p. 246)

Meaning is not in things but in between; in the iridescence, the interplay; in the interconnections; at the intersections, at the crossroads. Meaning is transitional as it is transitory; in the puns or bridges, the correspondence. (p. 247)

Meaning is new, or not at all; a new creation or not at all; poetry or not at all. The newness is the metaphor, or nonsense--saying one thing and meaning another. It is the legal fiction, which liberates from the letter of the law and from the tyranny of literal meaning. (p. 248)

Symbolism is polymorphous perversity, the translation of all of our senses into one another, the interplay between the senses, the metaphor, the free translation. The separation of the senses, their mutual isolation, is sensuality, is sexual organization, is bondage to the tyranny of one partial impulse, leading to the absolute and exclusive concentration of the life of the body in the representative person. (p. 249)

Polymorphously perverse sexuality, in and through every organ of perception:

> If in the morning sun I find it,
> there my eyes are fix'd/In happy
> copulation. (p. 249)

Knowledge is carnal knowledge. A subterranean passage between mind and body underlies all analogy, no word is metaphysical without its first being physical; and the body that is the measure of all things is sexual. All metaphors are sexual; a penis in every convex object and a vagina in every concave one. (pp. 249-50)

Every sentence is dialectics, an act of love. (p. 252)

Fusion: the distinction between inner self and outside world, between subject and object, overcome. To the enlightened man, the universe becomes his body: "You never enjoy the world aright till the Sea itself floweth in your veins, till you are clothed with the heavens and crowned with the stars." (pp. 253-54)

Symbolical consciousness, the erotic sense of reality, is a return to the principle of ancient animistic science, mystical participation, but now for the first time freely; instead of religion, poetry. (p. 254)

But the outcome of psychoanalysis of the discovery that magic and madness are everywhere, and dreams is what we are made of. The goal cannot be the elimination of magical thinking, or madness; the goal can only be conscious magic, or conscious madness; conscious mastery of these fires. And dreaming while awake. (p. 254)

Sleepers, awake. Sleep is separateness; the cave of solitude is the cave of dreams, the cave of the passive spectator. To be awake is to participate, carnally and not in fantasy, in the feast; the great communion. (p. 255)

Freedom means the resexualization of language so that our speaking is never abstract, cerebral, disembodied. Speech is embodied speech, the word-act, and to be embodied is to be sexual. The genuinely spoken stance is like a phallic thrust: properly spoken, in the right place. So language, like sex, and also like silence, can be a symbol for a mystical union between the self and the world, and between the self and others. Speaking and sexuality and silence: all acts of love. Can we learn to do it? If we can, then all reality becomes poetic rather than prosaic.

About silence, Chapter XVI, it is perhaps better that I hold my tongue. To those who listen, silence speaks. And if you have learned, your own commentaries excel mine.

V Symbolical Consciousness and a Choice

Love's Body, it seems to me, has many implications for the potential reunification of our badly fragmented culture. The book has implications for art and science and education and philosophy among other fields. But perhaps the religious implications appear to me the most significant of all.

Speaking personally, I do not any longer know how to believe in any one of the available religious traditions, and Marxism as it is ordinarily served up does not seem to me much better as an alternative. Yet our ordinary-common sensical-secular-empirical-scientific view of the world is sterile to my way of thinking. For me Brown shows a way that I can be religiously sensitive without being formally religious. He shows a way to transcend the forms, in other words, and in transcending the forms one can avoid being ensnared by the narrowness and dogmatism and literalism of each little religious tradition. *Love's Body* speaks to the possibility of what I have called polysymbolic religiosity, which I regard as a cultural development of considerable significance and which I have explored in my own writing. Brown is the herald of religiously eclectic polysymbolism. If, as I think, polysymbolism has developed into an important religious alternative in our society, that is reason enough to ask students to read and respond to *Love's Body*, and I shall continue to do so.

At the risk of succumbing to the academic literalism which has been one target of Brown's thought, I want to conclude my remarks by returning to Marcuse. If Marcuse has now more and more gone back to the Marxist type view that repression is overcome by socio-economic revolution and rearrangement, it is clear that there are deep, ineradicable differences with Brown's late, apocalyptic, deliberately visionary work. The controversy appeared in the February and March issues of *Commentary*, 1967 (and was reprinted in Marcuse's *Negations* [Beacon]): Marcuse criticizes *Love's Body* in his essay, "Love Mystified," and there is a reply by Brown. Put simply, Marcuse thinks that Brown has gone religious on him, and that has to be anathema for the Marxist due precisely to the reasons Marx gave, namely that it turns the attention of persons away from the apparent and pressing earthly problems before them to some other worldly sphere where, they are deluded to think, happiness will ultimately be found. At best then religion is disastrous for the revolution and earthly happiness; at worst it is a deliberate tool of the ruling classes to keep the lower classes in line, falling for the delusion of ultimate, non-worldly satisfaction--if happiness is to be gained in the future, unhappiness is bearable now, and therefore the inequitable status quo is legitimated. Marcuse attacks: "The radical destruction of history terminates in the religious tale, in which history is not synthesized but simply negated, abolished" (*Negations*, p. 232).

Attitudinal matters, as always, are not insignificant in this controversy. Marcuse, for all the latent Teutonic romanticism in him, just can't take Brown's fertile imagination seriously--at the very best it is totally irrelevant to the business at hand. "The airplane," he says, "is a penis symbol, but it also gets you in a couple of hours from Berlin to Vienna" (p. 235). As Marcuse states the crux of the disagreement: "The roots of repression are and remain real roots; consequently, their eradication remains a real and rational job. What is to be abolished is not the reality principle; not everything, but such particular things as business, politics, exploitation poverty. Short of this recapture of reality and reason, Brown's purpose is defeated, and the critical destruction of history, the discovery of its latent and real content, turns into the mystification of the latent and real content" (pp. 235-36). For Marcuse the obliteration of the common sense distinction between the real and the artificial, or we might say the common sense subject/object view of the world, is to leave the real world for the nether realms of irrelevant fantasy. Fusion between subject and object "would be the end of human life, in its instinctual as well as rational, unsublimated as well as sublimated, expression" (p. 238). And a final cruel rub for Marcuse is the symbolization or for him mystification of the revolution: "Revolution, freedom, fulfillment in turn become symbolic--symbolic goals and events. Symbolic of what? The answer remains, must remain, shrouded in mystery, because Brown envisions an Absolute, a Totality, a Whole which swallows up all parts and divisions, all tensions and all needs, that is to say, all life" (p. 241).

Brown in reply accepts Marcuse's interpretation of him, and even accepts the label mystification--from literalism to symbolism, the lesson, he says, of his life and the lesson which must be transmitted to the next generation. The fight has to be taken out of the realm of politics and into that of poetry; the world is not a collection of commodities; technology's meaning lies in its hidden relation to the body; genital organization must be overcome; chaos and fusion are the goals; the human form divinized. "And the language is the language not of reason but of love. Reason is power; powerful arguments; power-politics; *Realpolitik*; reality-principle. Love comes empty-handed; the eternal proletariat; like Cordelia, bringing Nothing" (*Negations*, pp. 246-47).

I leave you to make what you will of what finally comes down to a really stunning divergence between two men whose original stakes in Freud had been so similar and so profound--they have, as many, including Robinson, have noticed, quite simply developed in opposite directions, and one gets the feeling that despite the enlightenment they can bring to us, we are left with the same old classical dichotomy between reason, technique, social arrangements on the one hand, and intuitive, privatistic, other worldly mysticism on the other. Mankind's unhappy choice. Or is it really a choice that any of us can consciously make?